MILTON RESNICK

A Question of Seeing
Paintings 1959–1963

Essay by Nathan Kernan

Cheim & Read New York 2008

A QUESTION OF SEEING

NATHAN KERNAN

There is nothing physical about what I do. All I do is see, and make it possible to see more. Not less. I do that by breathing something on to canvas. I send a message of sorts… The message that I give [my work] is just to see — to make it possible to see.[1]

—Milton Resnick, 1972

It is the business of a painter not to contend with nature… but to make something out of nothing, in attempting which he must almost of necessity become poetical.[2]

—John Constable, 1824

The extraordinary paintings Milton Resnick made from 1959 to 1963 chart his moving from a more or less straightforward Abstract Expressionist mode toward the first, powerful expressions of the thickly-painted, near-monochrome works he became known for in the later 1960s, '70s and '80s. The narrative seems beautiful and self-evident, at least superficially. If we somehow distrust the bald verbalization of it, it may be partly because of Resnick's own marked distrust, expressed in many a talk and interview, of all facile terms and answers — or even basic ones, like the notion of cause and effect. "Abstract Expressionist" was a term he explicitly rejected (hating the fact that it pointed back to European Expressionism) along with "Action Painting" (which was originally a put-down) and any other formula cobbled together by critics after the fact to try to name the kind of painting he did from the 1940s on. "Paint," he said, "that's all I have. I only have paint."[3]

This span of years, 1959 to 1963, also happens to coincide with a time when the hard-won, short-lived "triumph" of New York Abstract Expressionism was giving way to upstart new movements. The period in the 1930s, '40s and early '50s when a small group of downtown artists acknowledged shared goals and a feeling of communal discovery was over. Pop Art, Minimalism and Color Field painting had arrived — even painterly figuration, rejuvenated by Abstract Expressionism, was experiencing a comeback — and for younger artists, Abstract Expressionism was just another style: take it or leave it. Whether or not Resnick was aware of these developments, this outpouring of remarkably large, glorious and untrammeled paintings just at this time seems both an apotheosis of Abstract Expressionism, and a transcendence of it. The heroic effort culminated in the astonishing, all white *New Bride*, a painting as beautiful and radical as any painting of its time. *New Bride*, in turn, set Resnick himself on a brave new path, developed out of Abstract Expressionism, not by rejecting it but by painting through it, holding to his lifelong aspiration simply and purely to see.

Milton Resnick was born Rachmiel Resnick in 1917, the year of the Russian Revolution, in the Ukrainian town of Bratslav. His family was Jewish, his grandfather and father successful builders. During his childhood civil war was raging and Resnick retained early memories of the marauding Red and White armies coming and going, of bodies lying in the streets. "They would pull people out and shoot them."[4] His father was of military age and went into hiding in nearby Odessa to avoid being pressed into service by either army. By bribing authorities and disguising themselves as peasants, the family, now including Resnick's sister Ethel, born in 1920, managed to escape and emigrate to America, via Romania, Paris and Cuba, in 1922. A second sister, Zelda, was born in Cuba in 1922.

They settled near relatives in Brooklyn, where Rachmiel entered public school. The teacher anglicized his name to Milton. Knowing no English, he spent First Grade sitting at the back of the room copying the alphabet. "I didn't know what it was, I only knew I had to make an A, B, C and make it stay on the same line...I never spoke to anybody. I had to stand up and I had to put my hand on my chest and everybody was talking and I would go 'blah, blah, blah.'"[5]

With some idea that he might follow his father into the building trade, Milton enrolled in the Hebrew Technical Institute on Astor Place to learn architectural drafting and lettering. But when he graduated, in 1932, the Depression had brought construction to a standstill. Milton had by then become interested in art and decided to go to Pratt Institute to become a commercial artist, "because that seemed a practical idea." A teacher there saw his drawings after Rembrandt etchings ("I didn't really like his paintings but I liked his drawings, his etchings, and I'd copy them"[6]) and recommended he transfer to a fine art school. He and a friend then both enrolled in the American Artists School in the fall of 1933. When his father learned that he intended to be a fine artist he kicked him out of the house. Cut off financially by his family, he became the elevator and errand boy at the School in exchange for tuition and a little room in the basement to paint in. He sold his blood, modeled, "did anything to keep alive."[7]

The American Artists School was one of several pre-War forcing-grounds for the future New York School. Despite an emphasis on Social Realism due to the school's close association with radical and Socialist causes, several semi-abstract painters, advanced for the time, like Stuart Davis, Max Weber and Francis Criss, taught there or were on the board (as was Meyer Shapiro). Ad Reinhardt was a fellow student. While he was at the American Artists School Resnick met Elaine Fried, who was studying at another art school. They became lovers and he persuaded her to transfer to the American Artists School. For a while, Resnick shared an apartment with Fried and her friend Ernestine Blumberg (later Lassaw).

Resnick often told a story of an encounter at the school with the painter Francis Criss. Resnick asked Criss, one of the few instructors he admired, to visit his small basement studio to see the painting he was working on, which was, he recalled, "a little like Soutine".[8] Criss came, and pointing to one detail in the painting said, "There's something wrong *here*." "And I said thanks, and he left," Resnick recalled. "And I painted that space out, and there was my picture. And the thing about that was that I was saving that little place. I thought that was the best place. So that's a very good lesson: always paint out the best place. It's like your ghost: you have to get at your ghosts and paint them out."[9]

After leaving the American Artists School, Resnick became part of a group of painters and friends living and working downtown that included Willem de Kooning, whom he met in 1938, Arshile Gorky, John Graham, Ibram Lassaw, Landes Lewitin and many others. It was a heady time in New York for painters; as Resnick said later, "It was something more or less in the air... we'd be carried by some wind."[10] Pat Passlof recalled (of the '40s) "There was a quickening: the sense that a day might make a difference."[11] "Everybody drank coffee and nobody had shows," remembered Edwin Denby. Artists would meet in the evenings at the Waldorf Cafeteria at Sixth Avenue and Eighth Street for long discussions about art—the forerunner of the post-War Artists' Club, of which

Resnick was a founding member. Resnick, like most, was still painting in a figurative mode in the '30s. His painting heroes were Cézanne and Soutine. A New York painter almost forgotten today, whose influence would show up later in Resnick's work, was Max Schnitzler, who was making very thickly painted abstractions in the '30s. For a short time in 1938, Resnick was on the easel painting division of the W.P.A. Federal Art Project.

The Second World War brought a shift in the perceived balance of power for New York artists vis-à-vis Europe, along with a stimulating influx of refugee artists. To Resnick it also brought an unwelcome hiatus from painting: in 1940, he was drafted and served in the US Army through most of the War, including the Normandy Landings. After returning to New York in 1945 he instantly caught up with what had gone on in his absence and began painting abstractions. There were strong family resemblances in these early post-War years between the work of Resnick and de Kooning, as one could see in small paintings by them both from 1945 and 1946, respectively, on view recently in the Metropolitan Museum as part of the Muriel Kallis Newman Bequest. In 1946 Resnick and de Kooning collaborated on painting *Labyrinth*, an enormous backdrop for a dance performance by Marie Marchowsky. De Kooning provided the original sketch, Resnick painted it to full size on canvas, and de Kooning "drew" in paint on top of that. The size—17 x 24 feet—foreshadows Resnick's later large paintings. De Kooning and Resnick's close relationship was further complicated by a romantic triangle that existed for a time between the two men and Elaine Fried, who would eventually marry de Kooning and become Elaine de Kooning.

From 1946 to 1948 Resnick lived in Paris, painting and ostensibly studying at the Academie Julien on the G.I. Bill. His studio on the Rue de Seine was next door to that of Wols and he became friendly with him and with Jean Hélion, Brancusi, Giacometti, among others. In a café the poet Tristan Tzara perspicaciously told him, "The trouble with you is you don't know that art is a commodity."[12] Unfortunately, all the canvases Resnick painted in Paris at this time were left behind with a friend and have been lost (though he did bring back a roll of works on paper). Commodity, indeed. When he returned to New York in the fall of 1948, de Kooning had also just returned from a summer teaching at Black Mountain College, bringing with him a young student of his, Pat Passlof. De Kooning introduced her to Resnick, calling him "the man he respected more than any other." She and Resnick would later become lovers and eventually marry.

By 1948, commercial attention was finally beginning to be paid to the downtown abstract painters, and de Kooning had his first solo exhibition (at the age of 44) at the Charles Egan Gallery. Egan scheduled a show for Resnick for 1949, took some paintings and sold them. There was a dispute, Resnick didn't get paid, and cancelled the show. Though he had been a much respected painter downtown since the late 30s: a central figure in discussions at the Waldorf Cafeteria, the Artists' Club and the Cedar Bar, and had helped organize the famous "Ninth Street Show" in 1951, Resnick's first solo show in New York, at the Poindexter Gallery, took place only in 1955. (It followed a solo exhibition at San Francisco's de Young Museum the same year, when he had been teaching at the University of California at Berkeley.) This relatively late debut has led some to mistakenly group him with the so-called "second generation" of Abstract Expressionists. Resnick himself did little to clarify matters by taking a principled stand against all such superficial comparisons and classifications, stating in 1962, "I am not an action painter. I am not an Abstract Expressionist. I am not younger than anybody or older..."[13]

Resnick had several shows in quick succession at Poindexter. In 1957, a feature article, "Resnick Paints a Picture" (part of a well-known series) appeared in *Art News* magazine. Resnick's painting from the mid-1940s through the mid-1950s was concerned in one way or another with interrelated shapes: smooth and biomorphic in the '40s; angular and gesturally painted in the '50s. His beautifully made abstractions of the mid-'50s are often expressed in a moody, earthy palette of browns, ochres, muddy greens, sharp reds, sour yellows. The shapes are fairly large, relative to the canvas, and often outlined or boxed in. Combating forms sometimes seem to exist in order to cancel each other out, to balance or draw attention from other forms which may be in danger of becoming too prominent, as though Resnick were heeding Criss's admonition to paint out the "best part." Thomas Hess emphasized their sense of balance when he wrote of them in *Art News*, "If Cubist paintings have armatures, Resnick's have musculatures: hard balances soft, tension implies equal and opposite relaxation…"[14]

Indeed, one could almost view Resnick's entire oeuvre as a working through of Francis Criss's well-remembered advice of the 1930s. That the artist's "favorite part" of a painting is exactly the part that needs to be obliterated from it is a radical, liberating, and unsettling idea. For Resnick it would lead to a constant self-questioning and a paradoxical situation in which the very idea of "success," however temporary or illusionary, became a kind of failure, or at least a sign to move on, to take things one step further. As he put it, "I wore out every conclusion I could come to." Resnick took no short-cuts: in order for the favorite part to be painted over, in order for the conclusion to be worn out, they had to have been there in the first place. Not always literally, for not every Resnick painting is an accumulation of pentimenti (though many are), but generally, in the overall arc of Resnick's career, where the "favorite part" took the form of the previous painting or body of work, which had to be passionately developed before it could be eradicated by new work. Every painting became a way of trying to vindicate, or retroactively justify, the previous one: a Sisyphean task, as Resnick realized. He said, "Half the time I thought: something's wrong. I can't understand it. And that's why I kept working, in a sense, so that I could somehow make up for what I've already wasted. To get to the point where if I could only see what I can do *now*, that can make what I've already done: some-thing. So it always seemed to me, I'm reaching but I'm never getting where I can make myself feel good about what I've done."[15]

In a way, the marks on a Resnick painting are replacements for marks that are not there: for the "ghost" that he speaks of having to paint out, or the color that he later speaks of having to "kill." There is a whiff of atavistic or Old Testament magic about this replacement or "killing" of one set of marks by another, as though the painting we see were a stand-in for another one that (like the name of Yahweh) cannot be "spoken," or had been sacrificed through an act of faith. For Resnick, though, it is not only the name of God that cannot be spoken, but the name of anything: a chair, an apple, a color. His impossible, Edenic ideal was that all visible phenomena must become nameless in order to be truly seen. Milton was not an observant Jew, yet his very love of talk, of parable, paradox and cryptic pronouncements, can seem to recall Talmudic disputation. "I love talk," Resnick told Geoffrey Dorfman. "The world is too large without talk."[16]

If there is almost a willful insistence on "images" in the clearly delineated rectangular shapes in paintings of the mid-fifties (such as *Model*, 1958), a partial eradication of images, in *Burning Bush* from 1959 and other paintings, is achieved by what looks like a painting over of them. There are still shapes, and the painting is still composed, to some extent, around relationships between them, but their boundaries are softened, and they have become less important than the overall field of brushstrokes they're now part of. The next step would be for the individual strokes of paint, instead of being used as elements to form — or eradicate — a shape, to themselves be, or replace, the shape.

The moody palette of *Burning Bush* allies it to the dark paintings that immediately preceded it; it is also one of the most Soutine-like paintings in Resnick's work. Its impassioned woozy movement and tactile brushstrokes, its browns, yellows and reds, seem to combine the hallucinatory weavings of Soutine's Cagnes landscapes with the carnality and firelight of his beef carcass paintings. The Old Testament title reinforces that connection, as it also suggests a metaphor for painting itself: as something alive and actively "burning" but never consumed; something which speaks to one and changes one's life.

Genie, painted in the same year, also seems like an apparition. Rather than being an allover composition, or having various incidents of more or less equal importance distributed across the surface, *Genie* presents one large, slightly darker, slightly more condensed form hovering in the center of a lighter, more openly painted field. Like another painting from the same year, *Column*, also in a vertical format, it plausibly evokes a floating column of cloud or smoke: a state of perpetual flux and insubstantiality. *Genie's* almost "feminine" palette of pink, yellow and light blue, the casual nonchalance and looseness of its marks, and the way they all seem to drift indecisively first in one direction then dart in another, make a striking contrast to the "muscular," dark, taut paintings of the mid-'50s. It is as though Resnick were trying not only to "paint out" that earlier body of work, but at the same time to make something as unlike what Thomas Hess liked about it as possible.

In 1959 Resnick was walking on lower Broadway when he saw a sign advertising a "5000 square foot light loft" for rent. It intrigued him: what did it mean, a "light loft"? The two words, "light" and "loft," seemed to speak directly, if cryptically, to the feeling of levitation he was ambitious for in his paintings. What did 5000 square feet look like? He went up and saw it. It had eight skylights and windows all the way across the front. "This is a dream. Oh, if I could only paint here." He decided to rent it for his studio. The sea-change that Resnick's work underwent in the years 1959 to 1962 is tied to the experience of this studio.

Actually, Resnick had already begun to paint large in his old studio on Tenth Street. At the end of the '50s, after sending most of his unsold paintings into storage, he was left with an empty studio and a wall ten feet high by fifteen feet wide. He decided to "paint a picture that big."[17] At first the problem seemed to be that he could not get back far enough from the painting to see what he was doing without constantly walking back and forth across the studio. However, he came to realize that his inability to take in the entire picture at once might actually be a good thing, "that it is not so much getting back to look at it, as how you work when you can't see it."[18] "The reason I painted those big paintings is that I couldn't see them…You only see what's right in front of you. There has to be a way in which you understand what you're doing when you can't see. So that has to be the feeling you can carry… To hold that feeling you have to give up something. You give up yourself. So that the painting is really not so much *you*, which a lot of people think, but the painting is *telling* you."[19] For Resnick, "seeing" became less an optical exercise than an act of willful "unlearning," or what he called "a suspension of belief." He tried explaining it this way: "Visually I know this glass. I give it a name. I can drink. There's something else about the glass and I don't know it… Let's say I don't even know what it is…You haven't given it a name, you haven't given it meaning, it doesn't speak for itself, you don't know. That's how I paint."[20]

The new 5000 square foot studio at 811 Broadway enabled Resnick to paint still bigger than 10 x 15 feet, and to work on several paintings at a time, as he liked to do. The paintings Resnick made there, with their approximate dimensions, include: *Swan*, 10 x 25 feet; *Tilt to the Land*, 10 x 16 feet, *East is the Place*, 10 x 16 feet, *Here I Remember*, 10 x 16 feet, *All Day Long*, 10 x 16 feet, *Mound*, 10 x 16 feet, *Ghost*, 10 x 16 feet, *Botany*, 8 1/2 x 14 1/2 feet, *Octave*, 8 x 10 feet, *Wheel*, 8 x 6 1/2 feet, and others.

The great size of these paintings is perhaps their most obvious characteristic, but not for that reason their least interesting one. Because of it, the paintings have a relationship not just to our eyes but our whole body, are "seen" bodily almost as much as optically. Their wide-screen format was carefully considered by Resnick not to exceed what could be encompassed in peripheral vision by a person standing close to them. We approach them warily, almost like early man venturing onto the unknown veldt. Several of their titles contain geographical references: *Tilt to the* Land, *East is the* Place, Here *I Remember*, as if the artist were reminding himself that the very size of these paintings makes them *places* in themselves—though not landscapes. "It isn't canvas that you approach for your focusing. It is a place," said Resnick. "And this place can be, by coincidence, where your canvas is.... A very important part of this whole thing lies in whether this canvas, which becomes this place—also becomes a world."[21]

To poet James Schuyler, writing in *Art News* about Resnick's 1960 show at Howard Wise Gallery, what was most striking about this group of paintings was the atomization, as it were, of imagery, which he associated with a joyful release: "The emblems and compositional structures are gone, he has revolutionized his style by concentrating on the smallest element, the stroke—in the name of joy or beauty."[22]

Tilt to the Land (1959) embraces chaos. Paint strokes go in every direction, are of every color, every density. There are areas where they are distinct from one another and allow bare canvas to show between them, areas where they are smudged together in opaque masses. It hasn't even the unity of disunity since there are still a few emblems: a red seed-like form, a rough green triangle, several blue darting passages. If it has a kind of order, it is the order of natural forces, of conflicting gravitational or magnetic fields around which masses seem to form and dissipate. It is like a universe, or a star nebula—the giant molecular clouds made of hydrogen and helium in which stars form. Though he meant it figuratively when he said the canvas must become a "world" or a "universe," his imagery often mirrors and reinforces that conceit. The painting's title may refer to the parable Resnick told at the Club in the '50s (and subsequently) in his "Message to Lionel Abel" about the early pilot who instinctively found a way of staying aloft flying through visually impenetrable clouds, when instruments alone would not keep him from falling. If the artist and the viewer are experiencing a "tilt to the land" it means we are in danger of falling; fear raises our adrenalin, as does this thrilling painting.

A "tilted" land has no horizon line, which may also link the title to Resnick's ideas about Cézanne. Resnick often described Cézanne's painting in terms of a "net," or a surface on which every square inch was "ticking"—continuous, that is, except that Cézanne was never able to do away with the horizon line, a "division" Resnick sought to eliminate in his own work. Cubism, he felt, misappropriated Cézanne's discoveries, in its concern with forms seemingly in front of or behind one another. Not believing in painted "space," Resnick wanted everything spread out on the surface: the long, vignetted central area of *Swan*, for example, might suggest something flayed—or an opened fan. If it's a "world" it's a Mercator projection, not a globe.

For some time Resnick had been (as he would continue to be) obsessed with what he described as getting his paintings to ascend or "rise." When he began to paint *Swan* (1961) in particular, he told himself, "I'm going to make it fly. So I called this picture *Swan*."[23] The imagery of *Swan*—surely one of the great unsung masterpieces of twentieth century American painting—again suggests floating cloud or nebula-like masses, or an elemental "becoming" that refuses to settle. Here as in other works, the formal dissipation of "emblems" into particulate strokes of paint can function as a image of the metamorphoses of elements in the physical world—water evaporating into air, solids burned to smoke. (A great mid-'50s painting, *Wannamaker*, was inspired by the spectacular fire that burned the former department store of that name near Astor Place in July, 1956.) To borrow the title of the 14th century mystical Christian text, it is a "Cloud of Unknowing," and as such, its imagery recapitulates Resnick's conviction that, "Art is not a learning process. It is the very reverse of learning. It is the unhinging of your soul from your sight."[24]

At 25 feet wide, *Swan* is the largest painting Resnick made before *Night* and *Day* in the late '80s. It is one of a group of paintings from this period (including *Octave*, *ASBW*, and *Wedding*) painted in a palette restricted to black, white, grey and occasionally some blue. The word "calligraphic" is a tricky one in talking of gestural painting, with its possible connotations of decorativeness and faux-orientalism (and Resnick had no particular interest in Chinese or Japanese painting) but in *Swan* more than in other paintings the separate strokes of which the painting is composed take on individual identities, turning into scribbles and curlicues and long trailing verticals which, here and there, do seem faintly reminiscent of Chinese running script. The cursive writing of *Swan* gives the painting a discursive quality, a trait shared, perhaps, with Cy Twombly's more literally written scribbles. Both painters transmute Abstract Expressionist gesture into a highly personal, uncomposed, and somewhat obsessive recording of inner sensation, which one might also compare, in this regard, to Henri Michaux's mescaline drawings, with their fevered appearance of being readouts of the activity of his nervous system. The written character of some of the marks in *Swan* remind us that Resnick (like Michaux) was also a poet, and that later in this same year, 1961, he published two books of poems, *Up and Down* and the three-part *Journal of Voyages*.

The burst of energy and inspiration in which in this extraordinary group of paintings was created did not come without personal cost. In 1961 Resnick suffered what he described as a breakdown: "I thought I was going to die and I had to stop painting, and bought new suits and walked around like I was not a painter any more."[25] He gave up the Broadway studio, married his longtime companion Pat Passlof, and together they went to France. After a few months they returned to New York, where Resnick took a studio on Spruce Street near City Hall, an area where at the time no artists had yet thought to live or work. He did not know how or whether to begin painting again, but he did begin, telling himself he had to "learn how to paint… begin all over again." He had another giant canvas, 9 x 17 1/2 feet, and the first thing he did was paint it entirely blue. "And then I thought, Well I don't like blue, I'll make it white, and so I bought a hundred tubes of Permalba white, and then I just squeezed it on and brushed it on, and just any old thing. And then it seemed to me that I was doing something but I wasn't sure what it was, but I needed more white, so I bought another hundred tubes and another hundred tubes, and then it seemed to me that I couldn't take my eye off the picture because if I did I'd fall. So I used to take the cap off the tube and throw it on the floor and step on it, and then reach down with the brush to paint with. And finally I stopped…"[26] and that painting, which Resnick continued to work on until 1963, was *New Bride*, now in the collection of the Smithsonian American Art Museum in Washington, DC.

After forty-five years, *New Bride* has lost none of its breathtaking audacity or austere beauty. In its presence we are convinced that it was created out of necessity: emotional, physical and inevitable, rather than (say) intellectual curiosity. It anticipates by some years Robert Ryman's monochromatic, unfigured white paintings, and while the similarity to that work may be tangential, both artists share an engagement with the painting as a "concrete" object, with extreme subtleties of surface, with paint itself, and with the act of seeing. Sounding a bit like Resnick, Ryman wrote in 1975, "What is done with paint is the essence of all painting. I am not talking of the technical processes of painting, which in itself is important, but of the seeing of painting. This 'seeing' can be so complex that the possibilities for painting are endless."[27]

In *New Bride, Wedding* and the paintings that would follow, Resnick followed Francis Criss's advice—and arguably the Abstract Expressionist impulse as well—to its logical, radical conclusion: the elimination of all, or apparently all, imagery. "You put [down] shapes and they become familiar. And I spent a long time thinking, I don't *want* those shapes, why are they there?... and if you know something about my work you know that those shapes just fell apart. Little by little, I ate away the shape…so that now I have no shape, no lines—*paint* that's all I have. I only have paint."[28]

For the next twenty-five years, Resnick painted more or less "monochromatic" works which were never, in fact, monochromatic, but were composed of as many colors as one could imagine, resolving into the impression of a single predominant hue. In these radical and romantic paintings, without "movement, motion or time," Resnick's preoccupation with the physical matter of paint is most explicit. A decade or so before his death in 2004, with perhaps a final, inverted nod to Francis Criss's long-ago advice, Resnick made a surprising and poignant return to imagery—sometimes figural imagery at that—the very thing he had worked so single-mindedly to eliminate.

Resnick's late monochromatic work seems very "physical." The viewer is exceedingly aware of the thickness of the paint on the canvas, its rough and topographical texture, its probable weight, the obsessive, dogged work that went into it. So it is all the more beautiful and jolting to read Resnick's words from an interview with Geoffrey Dorfman (quoted at the head of this essay) saying that "there is nothing physical" about what he does, and that all he does is "breathe" onto canvas. It's true, though, that Resnick's paintings sometimes do give the illusion that they are actually floating a few inches in front of where you know the canvas to be. They may weigh up to hundreds of pounds, but in the seeing they are as a breath of air.

NOTES

[1] Geoffrey Dorfman, *Out of the Picture: Milton Resnick and the New York School*. New York: Midmarch Arts Press, 2003. p. 205.
[2] Quoted by Conal Shields in *Constable's Skies*, edited by Frederic Bancroft. New York: Salander-O'Reilly Galleries, 2004 (exhibition catalogue). p. 117
[3] Transcription of a public interview with Milton Resnick and B. C. Holland at the School of the Art Institute of Chicago, April 25, 1988, unpublished. (Hereafter "Chicago.") p. 10
[4] Milton Resnick, in conversation with the author, December 11, 1997, and subsequently.
[5] ibid.
[6] ibid.
[7] Dorfman, op. cit., p 14
[8] ibid., p 17
[9] Chicago, op. cit., p. 1
[10] Dorfman, op. cit., pp. 187-188
[11] ibid., p 276
[12] Chicago, op. cit. p. 5
[13] Quoted in Linda L. Cathcart, *Milton Resnick Paintings 1945-1985*, Houston: Contemporary Arts Museum, 1985 (exhibition catalogue), p. 83

[14] ibid., p. 79
[15] Chicago, op. cit., p. 15
[16] Dorfman, op. cit., p. 71
[17] ibid., p. 81
[18] ibid., p. 83
[19] Chicago, op. cit., p. 11
[20] ibid., p. 5
[21] Dorfman, op. cit., p. 142
[22] James Schuyler, *Selected Art Writings* (edited by Simon Pettet), Santa Rosa: Black Sparrow Press, 1998. p. 184
[23] Dorfman, op. cit., p. 182
[24] ibid., p. 154
[25] Chicago, op. cit., p. 13
[26] ibid., pp. 13-14
[27] Quoted in Gary Garrels, *Robert Ryman*, New York: Dia Art Foundation, 1988 (exhibition catalogue), p. 24
[28] Chicago, op. cit., p. 10

BURNING BUSH 1959

Oil on canvas 63 x 48 in 160 x 121.9 cm
Collection Museum of Modern Art, New York, Larry Aldrich Foundation Fund, 1959.
Accession Number: 612.1959

Y + R 1958
Oil on canvas 67 x 68 in 170.2 x 172.7 cm

Y + R 1958 (detail)

Oil on canvas 67 x 68 in 170.2 x 172.7 cm

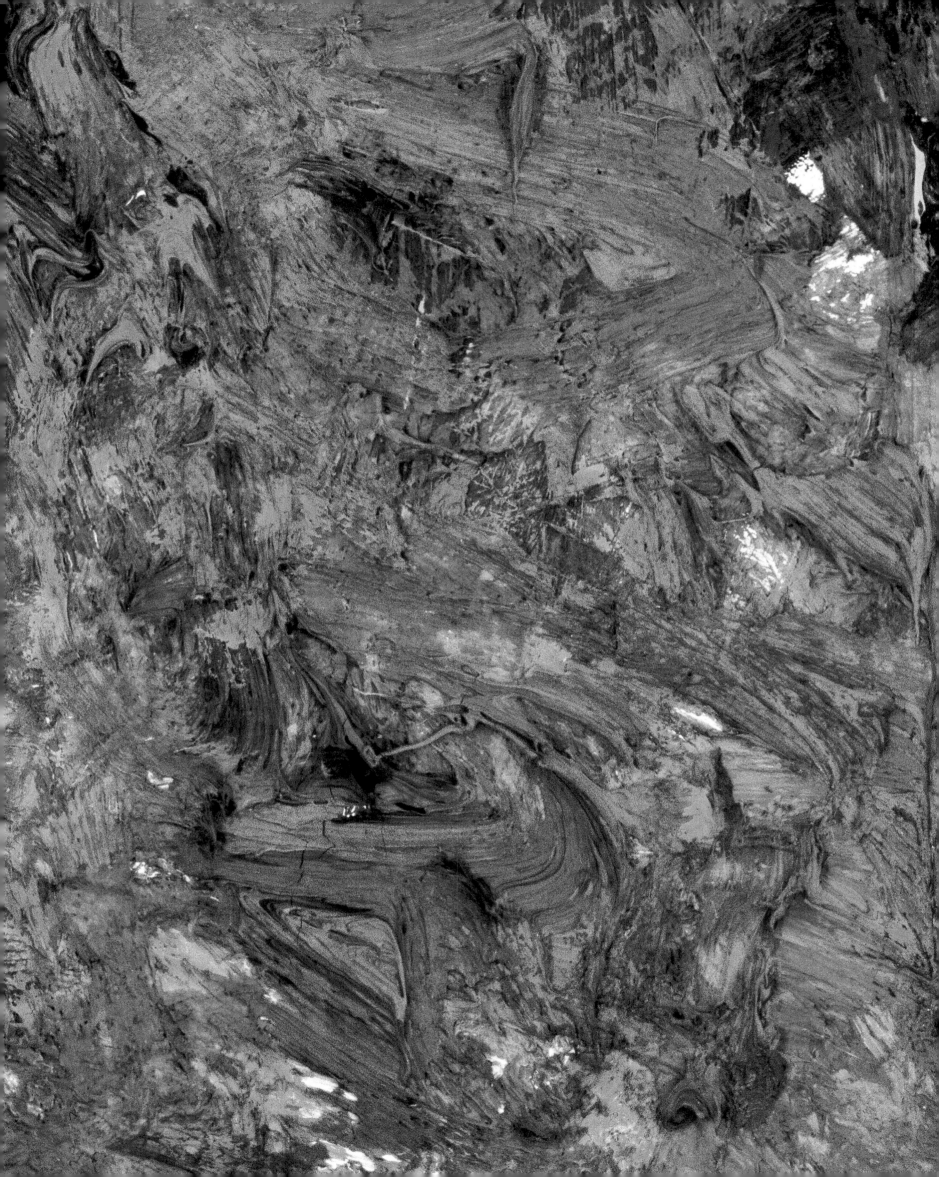

AS.2 1959
Oil on canvas 82 x 80 in 208.3 x 203.2 cm

UNTITLED 1959

Oil on canvas 70 x 49 3/4 in 177.8 x 126.4 cm

GENIE 1959

Oil on canvas 104 x 70 in 264.2 x 177.8 cm

Collection Whitney Museum of American Art, New York, Purchase 60.31

GENIE 1959 (detail)

Oil on canvas 104 x 70 in 264.2 x 177.8 cm

Collection Whitney Museum of American Art, New York, Purchase 60.31

UNTITLED 1959

Oil on canvas 35 x 23 in 88.9 x 58.4 cm

TILT TO THE LAND 1959

Oil on linen 104 1/4 x 190 1/4 in 264.8 x 483.2 cm (detail, following page)

Collection John D. Kahlbetzer

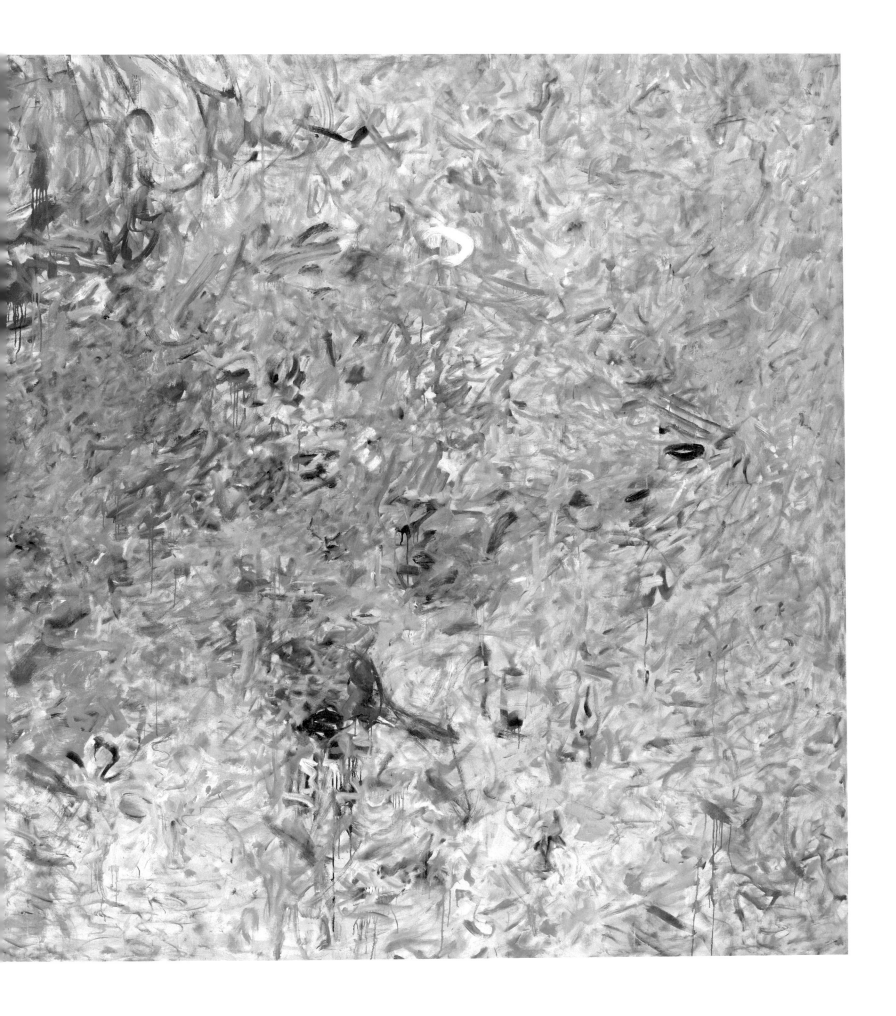

SWAN 1961

Oil on canvas 116 3/4 x 273 5/8 in 296.5 x 695 cm

Collection of the Modern Art Museum of Fort Worth, Museum Purchase,
The Benjamin J. Tillar Memorial Trust.

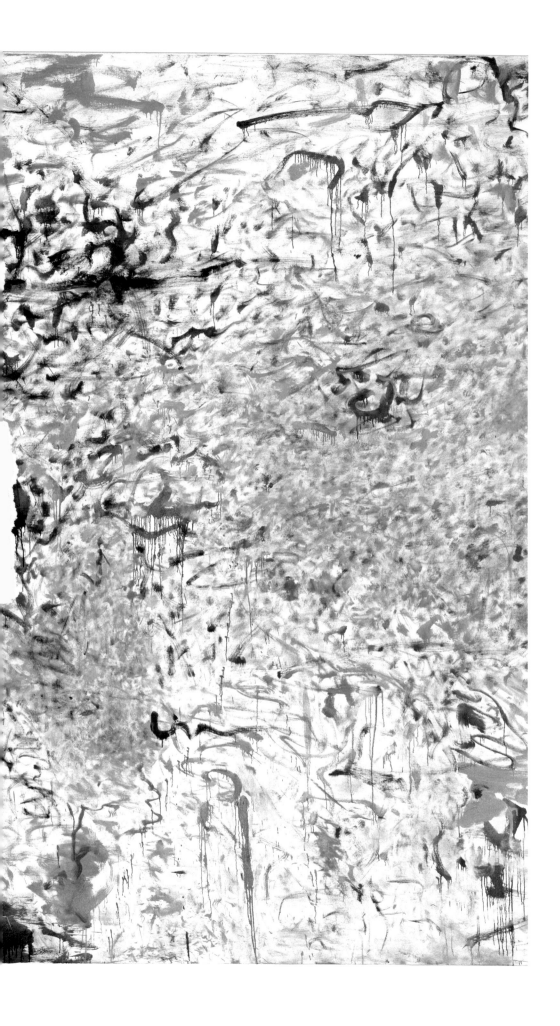

SWAN 1961 (detail)

Oil on canvas   116 3/4 x 273 5/8 in   296.5 x 695 cm
Collection of the Modern Art Museum of Fort Worth, Museum Purchase,
The Benjamin J. Tillar Memorial Trust.

EAST IS THE PLACE 1959
Oil on canvas 117 x 190 in 297.2 x 482.6 cm
Collection Milwaukee Art Museum; Gift of Mr. and Mrs. Howard Wise, New York.

EAST IS THE PLACE 1959 (detail)

Oil on canvas 117 x 190 in 297.2 x 482.6 cm
Collection Milwaukee Art Museum; Gift of Mr. and Mrs. Howard Wise, New York.

MOUND 1961

Oil on canvas 115 x 185 in 292.1 x 469.9 cm
Collection National Gallery of Art, Washington, DC

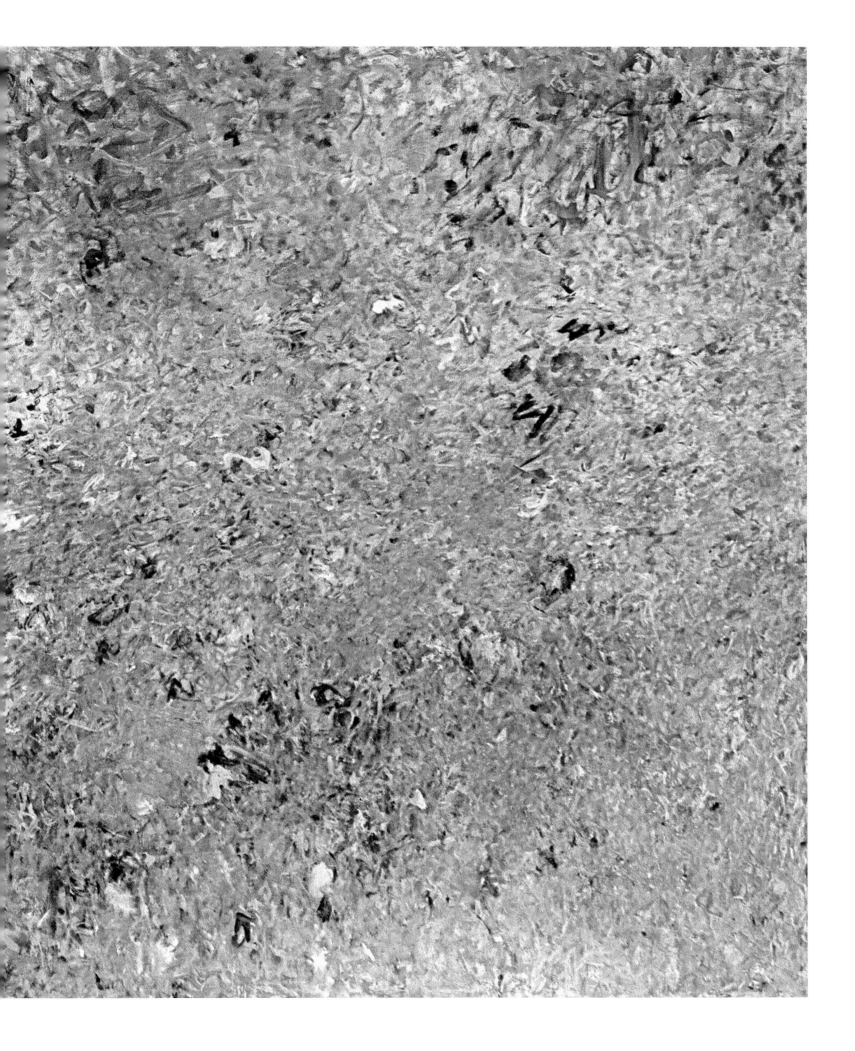

WEDDING 1962

Oil on canvas 108 3/4 x 102 5/8 in 276.2 x 260.7 cm
Collection Metropolitan Museum of Art

NEW BRIDE 1963

Oil on canvas 109 1/8 x 210 1/2 in 277.2 x 534.7 cm

Collection National Museum of American Art, Smithsonian Institution, Gift of Vincent Melzac.

BIOGRAPHY

1917	Born Bratslav, Ukraine, January 7
1922	Immigrated to the United States
2004	Died New York, March 12

EDUCATION

1932	Pratt Institute
1933–37	American Artists School
1938–39	Worked for W.P.A. Art Project
1940–45	Military Service, U.S. Army
1946–48	Lived and painted in Paris

SOLO EXHIBITIONS

2008	*Milton Resnick: A Question of Seeing: Paintings 1959–1963*, Cheim & Read, New York
2006	*Milton Resnick: The Life of Paint*, The Anthony Giordano Gallery, Dowling College, Oakdale, New York
	Black & Blue, Robert Miller Gallery, New York
2005	*Milton Resnick: Late Works*, New York Studio School, New York
2002	*Milton Resnick Five Years: 1959–1963*, Robert Miller Gallery, New York
2001	*Milton Resnick: X Space*, Robert Miller Gallery, New York
2000	Nielsen Gallery, Boston
1997	*Milton Resnick Monuments*, Robert Miller Gallery, New York
1996	*Recent Paintings*, Robert Miller Gallery, New York
1995	*Recent Paintings*, Robert Miller Gallery, New York
1992	Robert Miller Gallery, New York *The Substance of Painting: Part I Milton Resnick: New Paintings on Paper & Panel*, d.p. Fong and Spratt Galleries, San Jose, California
1991	*Milton Resnick: Straws 1981–1982*, Robert Miller Gallery, New York
1988	Daniel Weinberg Gallery, Los Angeles Robert Miller Gallery, New York
1987	Galerie Montenay–Delsol, Paris Meredith Long Gallery, Houston CompassRose Gallery, Chicago
1986	*Arbeiten auf Papier*, Galerie Biedermann, Munich Robert Miller Gallery, New York Gallery Urban, Nagoya, Japan
1985	Robert Miller Gallery, New York *Milton Resnick: Paintings 1945–1985*, Museum of Contemporary Art, Houston (traveled to University

Art Museum, California State University, Long Beach)
Hand in Hand Galleries, New York
Meredith Long Gallery, Houston, Texas

1983   Gruenebaum Gallery, New York
                Main Gallery, Art Department, San Jose State University, San Jose, California

1982   Max Hutchinson Gallery, New York

1980   Max Hutchinson Gallery, New York

1979   Max Hutchinson Gallery, New York
                Robert Miller Gallery, New York

1977   Max Hutchinson Gallery, New York

1975   Poindexter Gallery, New York

1973   Kent State University Art Galleries, Kent State University, Kent, Ohio

1972   Max Hutchinson Gallery, New York

1971   Roswell Museum and Art Center, New Mexico

1969   Arden Anderson Gallery, Edgartown, Massachusetts

1968   Reed College, Portland, Oregon

1967   Madison Art Center, Madison, Wisconsin

1964   Howard Wise Gallery, New York
                Feiner Gallery, New York

1963   Zabriskie Gallery, Provincetown, Massachusetts

1962   Feiner Gallery, New York

1961   Howard Wise Gallery, New York

1960   Howard Wise Gallery, Cleveland, Ohio
                Howard Wise Gallery, New York

1959   Ellison Gallery, Fort Worth, Texas
                Holland-Goldowsky Gallery, Chicago
                Poindexter Gallery, New York
                American Association of University Women of Rochester, New York

1957   Poindexter Gallery, New York

1955   The Fine Arts Museums of San Francisco, M.H. de Young Memorial Museum & California Palace of the
                Legion of Honor, San Francisco

GROUP EXHIBITIONS

2007   *Abstract Expressionism and Other Modern Works: The Muriel Kallis Steinberg Newman Collection in the*
                Metropolitan Museum of Art, Metropolitan Museum of Art, New York
                Significant Form, The Persistence of Abstraction, Maly Manege State Exhibition Hall, Moscow

2006   *1950 to Now: Works from the Collection*, Museum of Fine Arts, St. Petersburg, Florida

2005	*The Continuous Mark: 40 Years of the New York Studio School: Part 2 (1971–1978)*, New York Studio School, New York
2004	*Ground—Field—Surface*, Robert Miller Gallery, New York
2001-03	*The Stamp of Impulse: Abstract Expressionist Prints*, Worcester Art Museum, Worcester; Massachusettes exhibition traveled to The Cleveland Museum of Art, Cleveland; Amon Carter Museum, Fort Worth; Mary and leigh Block Museum of Art, Northwestern University, Evanston, Illinois
2001-02	*Monet un die Moderne (Monet and Modernism)*, Kunsthalle, Munich; exhibition traveled to Fondation Beyeler, Basel/Riehen
2001	*A Winter Group of Artist Couples*, Katharina Rich Perlow Gallery, New York *176th Annual Exhibition*, National Academy of Design, New York
2000-01	*Excavating Abstract Expressionism*, Auditorio de Galicia, Santiago de Compostela, Spain
2000	*Nature: Contemporary Art and the Natural World*, Contemporary Gallery, Marywood University, Scranton, Pennsylvania *Painting Abstraction*, New York Studio School of Drawing, Painting and Sculpture, New York
1999-2001	*Art in America: 2000*, Art in Embassies Program, Ambassadorial Residence to the Slovak Republic
1999-2000	*The American Century: Art & Culture 1950–2000*, Whitney Museum of American Art, New York *Painters/Painters*, Frederick Spratt Gallery (in association with Larry Evans/James Willis Gallery), San Francisco; exhibition traveled to Frederick Spratt Gallery, San Jose
1999	*Material Abstraction*, Kingsborough Community College of CUNY Art Gallery, Brooklyn; coordinated exhibition with Elizabeth Harris Gallery, New York
1997	*The Figure Revisited*, The Gallery at Hastings-On-Hudson, New York *After the Fall: Aspects of Abstract Painting Since 1970*, Snug Harbor Cultural Center, Staten Island, New York
1996	*Abstract Expressionism in the United States*, Centro Cultural Arte Contemporaneo, Mexico City, Mexico *Summer Group Show*, Robert Miller Gallery, New York
1995	*1995 Biennial Exhibition*, Whitney Museum of American Art, New York *10 + 10*, New York Studio School, New York *Action and Edge: 1950s and 1960s*, Katharina Rich Perlow Gallery, New York *The Small Painting*, O'Hara Gallery, New York
1994	*Paths of Abstraction: Painting in New York 1944–1981, Selections from the Ciba Art Collection*, Bertha and Karl Leubsdorf Art Gallery, Hunter College, New York *Abstract Works on Paper*, Robert Miller Gallery, New York *With a Passage of Time*, Vanderwoude Tananbaum Gallery, New York *Reclaiming Artists of the New York School: Toward a More Inclusive View of the 1950s*, Sidney Mishkin Gallery, Baruch College, The City University of New York, New York *Isn't it Romantic?*, curated by Michael Walls, On Crosby Street, New York *The Shaman as Artist/The Artist as Shaman*, Aspen Art Museum, Colorado
1993	*Star Zone*, Bondie's Contemporary Art, New York *Timely & Timeless*, The Aldrich Museum of Contemporary Art, Ridgefield, Connecticut *The Inaugural Show*, The Painting Gallery, New York *Windows and Doors*, Holly Solomon Gallery, New York *The Usual Suspects*, Manny Silverman Gallery, Los Angeles *Exhibition of Work by Newly Elected Members and Recipients of Honors and Abstract–Figurative Awards*, American Academy and Institute of Arts and Letters, New York Robert Miller Gallery, New York

1992	*Important Works on Paper*, Meredith Long & Company, Houston
	Summer Group Exhibition, Ginny Williams Gallery, Denver
	Painters, Trenkmann Gallery, New York
	Paint, Edward Thorp Gallery, New York
	Paths to Discovery The New York School: Works on Paper from the 1950s and 1960s, curated by Ellen Russotto, Sidney Mishkin Gallery, Baruch College, City University of New York
	Al Held and Milton Resnick 1955–1965, Manny Silverman Gallery, Los Angeles
1991	*Painting*, Galerie Lelong, New York
	The New York School: Works on Paper from the Fifties & Sixties, Elston Fine Arts, New York
	Contemporary Abstract Paintings: Resnick, Reed, Laufer & Moore, Muscarelle Museum of Art, College of William and Mary, Williamsburg, Virginia
1990	*Line & Action*, Tavelli Gallery, Aspen, Colorado
	Group Exhibition, Manny Silverman Gallery, Los Angeles
	Changing Perceptions: The Evolutions of Twentieth Century American Art, Weatherspoon Art Gallery, University of North Carolina, Greensboro, North Carolina
	Forty-second Annual Academy-Institute Purchase Exhibition, American Academy and Institute of Arts and Letters, New York
	Some Seventies Works, Robert Miller Gallery, New York
	The Figure in the 20th Century, Meredith Long & Co., Houston
	Works by Newly Elected Members and Recipients of Awards, American Academy and Institute of Arts and Letters, New York
	Academy-Institute Invitational Exhibition of Painting and Sculpture, American Academy and Institute of Arts and Letters, New York
	The Image of Abstract Paintings in the 1980s, Rose Art Museum, Brandeis University, Waltham, Massachusetts
1989	*Envoys*, New York Studio School, New York
	Forty-first Annual Purchase Exhibition, American Academy and Institute of Arts and Letters, New York
	The Gestural Impulse 1945–1960, Whitney Museum of American Art (Federal Reserve Plaza), New York
	Exhibition of Masterworks, Riva Yares Gallery, Scottsdale, Arizona
	A Decade of American Drawing 1980–1989, Daniel Weinberg Gallery, Los Angeles
	Selections from the Collection of Marc and Livia Strauss, Aldrich Museum of Contemporary Art, Ridgefield, Connecticut
	Abstraction as Landscape, Gallery Urban, New York
1988	*Recent Painterly Paintings*, Schreiber/Cutler, Inc., New York
1987	*Works on Paper, Beijing Art Institute*, Beijing, China (traveled to Shanghai Art Museum, China; Alisan Gallery, Hong Kong; Newhouse Center For Contemporary Art, Snug Harbor Cultural Center, Staten Island, New York; Nielsen Gallery, Boston
	The Presence of Nature: Some American Paintings, Barbara Krakow Gallery, Boston
	After Pollock: Three Decades of Diversity, Iannetti Lanzone Gallery, San Francisco
	Black, Siegeltuch Gallery, New York
	American Still Life 1980–87, Meredith Long & Co., Houston
	Post Abstract Expressionism, Vanderwonde Tananbaum Gallery, New York
	Modern: Contemporary Masters, Lever/Meyerson Galleries, New York
	Inner Worlds, Sarah Lawrence College Art Gallery, Bronxville, New York
1986	*Portraits*, New York Studio School of Drawing, Painting and Sculpture, New York
	The 1950s American Artists in Paris, Part III, Denise Cade Gallery, New York
	Monotypes, Oscarsson Siegeltuch, New York
	Summer Group Show, Robert Miller Gallery, New York
	Absolutes Defined: Line, Light and Surface, Oscarsson Siegeltuch, New York
	Portraits and Self-Portraits, Sorkin Gallery, New York
	Heads, Mokotoff Gallery, New York
	Naked Paint, Newhouse Gallery, Snug Harbor Cultural Center, Staten Island, New York
1985	*The Gathering of the Avant Garde: The Lower East Side, 1950–70*, Kenkelba House, Inc., New York

Group Show, Art Galaxy, New York
Masters of the Fifties American Abstract Painting from Pollock to Stella, Marisa Del Re Gallery, New York

1984
Group Show, Hand in Hand Galleries, New York
Salvo, Siegel Contemporary Art, New York
Summer Group Show, Robert Miller Gallery, New York
1 + 1 = 2, Bernice Steinbaum Gallery, New York
Summer Group Show, Max Hutchinson Gallery, New York
Group Show, Art Galaxy, New York
Beauties & Beasts, Pratt Manhattan Center Gallery, Pratt Institute, New York

1983
New York to Bennington, Bennington College, New York
Paintings of the 1970s, Queens College, New York
Summer Group Show, Max Hutchinson Gallery, New York
Purism, Segal Gallery, New York
Vintage New York, Contemporary Art at One Penn Plaza, One Penn Plaza, New York
Paint as Image, Max Hutchinson Gallery, New York

1982
Four Painters, Art Galaxy, New York
Synergy/Artists 1+1=3, Thorpe Intermedia Gallery, Sparkhill, New York
Tenth Anniversary Exhibition of Major Paintings, Drawings and Sculpture, Gruenebaum Gallery, New York

1981
1981 Painting Invitational, Oscarsson-Hood Gallery, New York
Art for Your Collection, Museum of Art, Rhode Island School of Design, Providence, Rhode Island
Abstract Expressionism From the Michener Collection, Abilene Fine Arts Museum, Abilene, Texas
For Love and Money: Dealers Choose I, Pratt Manhattan Center Gallery, Pratt Institute, New York (traveled
to Hartwick College Museums, Oneonta, New York)
CIBA-GEIGY Collects: Aspects of Abstraction, Sewall Art Gallery, Rice University, Houston
An American Choice: The Muriel Kallis Steinberg Newman Collection, Metropolitan Museum of Art,
New York

1980
Luminosity in Paint, Landmark Gallery, New York

1978
American Painting of the 1970s, Albright-Knox Art Gallery, Buffalo, New York (traveled)
Recent Works on Paper by Contemporary American Artists, Madison Art Center, Madison, Wisconsin
In the Realm of the Monochromatic: 17 Painters, Susan Caldwell Gallery, New York

1977
Critic's Choice: A Loan Exhibition from the New York Gallery Season, 1976–77, The Joe & Emily Lowe Art
Gallery, College of Visual and Performing Arts, Syracuse University, Syracuse, New York

1976
Works on Paper from the CIBA-GEIGY Collection, Wichita Falls Museum and Art Center,
Wichita Falls, Kansas
Around 10th Street: Abstract Expressionism in the 1950s, Young-Hoffman Gallery, Chicago
From Foreign Born American Masters, Milwaukee Art Center, Milwaukee
*Abstract Expressionists and Imagists: A Retrospective View and Exhibition of Paintings from the Michener
Collection*, Archer M. Huntington Gallery, University of Texas at Austin

1974
Works on Paper from CIBA-GEIGY Collection, Summit Art Center, Summit, New Jersey
The 1960s: Color Painting in the United States from the Michener Collection, University Art Museum, The
University of Texas at Austin
Frank O'Hara, A Poet Among Painters, Whitney Museum of American Art, New York
Five American Painter's Recent Work: De Kooning, Mitchell, Motherwell, Resnick, Tworkov, The Art Galleries,
University of California, Santa Barbara

1973
Group Show, Gallery A, Sydney, Australia
Works on Paper, Max Hutchinson Gallery, New York
Group Show, Landmark Gallery, New York
American Art at Mid-Century I, National Gallery of Art, Washington, DC
Abstract Expressionism: The First and Second Generations, Selected from Paintings in the Michener
Collection, University Art Museum, University of Texas at Austin
Visual R&D: A Corporation Collects: The CIBA-GEIGY Collection of Contemporary Paintings, University Art

Museum, University of Texas at Austin
Selections from the New York University Collection, William Benton Museum, University of Connecticut, Storrs, Connecticut
1973 Biennial Exhibition, Whitney Museum of American Art, New York

1972   *The Michener Collection: American Paintings of the 20th Century Inaugural Exhibition in the Michener Galleries*, University of Texas at Austin

1971   *A New Consciousness: The CIBA-GEIGY Collection*, Hudson River Museum, Yonkers, New York
American Paintings of the Sixties from the Michener Collection, Tyler Museum of Art, University of Texas
20th Century Painting and Sculpture from the New York University Art Collection, Hudson River Museum, Yonkers, New York
American Social Realism Between the Wars from the Michener Collection, University of Texas Art Galleries, Austin

1970   *Selections from the Vincent Melzac Collection*, Corcoran Gallery of Art, Washington, DC

1969   *The New American Painting and Sculpture: The First Generation*, Museum of Modern Art, New York
Group Show, Bundy Gallery, Waitsfield, Vermont

1968   *American Paintings: The 1950s*, Georgia Museum of Art, The University of Georgia, Athens, (traveled to Wichita Art Museum, Kansas; Charles and Emma Frye Art Museum, Seattle; Roberson Memorial Center for the Arts & Sciences, Binghamton, New York; University of Pittsburgh; The Huntington National Bank, Columbus, Ohio; Edmonton Art Gallery)
American Abstract Expressionists from the Michener Foundation Collection, Millersville State College, Pennsylvania
The Neuberger Collection: An American Collection of Paintings, Drawings and Sculpture I, (traveled to National Gallery of Fine Arts, Smithsonian Institute, Washington, DC)
The Neuberger Collection: An American Collection of Paintings, Drawings and Sculpture I, Museum of Art, Rhode Island School of Design, Providence and Annmary Brown Memorial, Brown University, Providence, Rhode Island
Painting as Painting, University Art Museum, University of Texas at Austin

1967   *1967 Annual Exhibition of Contemporary Painting*, Whitney Museum of American Art, New York
Contemporary Paintings from the Michener Foundation Collection, Old Dominion College, Norfolk, Virginia
Selections from the Michener Foundation Collection, Perkiomen School, Pittsburgh
Large Scale American Paintings, Jewish Museum, New York

1966   *Twentieth Century American Painters from the Michener Foundation Collection*, Ursinus College, Collegeville, Pennsylvania
New Acquisitions 1963-66, The James A. Michener Foundation Collection, Allentown Art Museum, Allentown, Pennsylvania
One Hundred and Sixty First Annual Exhibition of American Painting and Sculpture, Pennsylvania Academy of Fine Arts, Philadelphia

1965   *Expressionism of the Fifties*, Kansas City Art Institute, Kansas City, Missouri
79 Painters Who Paint, Poindexter Gallery; Graham Gallery; Martha Jackson Gallery; Kornblee Gallery; Grace Borgenicht Gallery, New York (simultaneous exhibitions)

1964   *Group Show*, The Gallery of Modern Art, Scottsdale, Arizona
New Accessions, U.S.A., Colorado Springs Fine Arts Center, Colorado
Recent American Paintings, University Art Museum, the University of Texas at Austin

1963   *Annual Exhibition 1963, Contemporary American Painting*, Whitney Museum of American Art, New York
American Impressionists: Two Generations, Fort Lauderdale Art Center, Fort Lauderdale, Florida
Directions–American Paintings, San Francisco Museum of Art, San Francisco

1962   *The Closing Show*, Tanager Gallery, New York
Art: USA Now–The Johnson Collection of Contemporary American Paintings, Milwaukee Art Center, Wisconsin
Contemporary Art in Cleveland Collections, Cleveland Museum of Art, Ohio

Art Since 1950: America and International, Seattle World's Fair, Seattle
Tenth Street, 1952, Tanager Gallery, New York
One Hundred and Fifty Seventh Annual Exhibition of American Painting and Sculpture, Pennsylvania
Academy of Fine Arts, Philadelphia
65th American Exhibition: Some Directions in Contemporary Painting and Sculpture, The Art
Institute of Chicago

1961   *Pan–American Exhibition of Contemporary Painting,* United States Information Agency
(traveling exhibition)
American Vanguard Exhibition of Contemporary American Painting, United States Information Agency
(traveling exhibition)
Group Show, Michigan State University, East Lansing, Michigan
Annual Exhibition of 1961, Contemporary American Painting, Whitney Museum of American Art, New York
Contemporary Paintings Selected from 1960–1961 New York Gallery Exhibitions, Yale University Art Gallery,
New Haven, Connecticut
American Abstract Expressionists and Imagists, Solomon R. Guggenheim Museum, New York
The Face of the Fifties, Recent Painting and Sculpture From the Collection of the Whitney Museum of Art,
University of Michigan Museum of Art, Ann Arbor, Michigan

1960   *Group Show,* Tanager Gallery, New York
An Exhibition of Modern American Painting and Sculpture, Kroeber Hall, University of California, Berkeley
The Horace Richter Collection: Contemporary American Painting and Sculpture, Mint Museum of Art,
Charlotte, North Carolina
60 American Painters–Abstract Expressionists Painting of the Fifties, Walker Art Center, Minneapolis
Contemporary American Painting, Columbus Gallery of Fine Art, Ohio

1959   *1959 Annual Exhibition: Contemporary American Paintings,* Whitney Museum of American Art, New York
Milton Resnick/Edward Dugmore, Allyn Gallery, Southern Illinois University, Carbondale, Illinois
Milton Resnick Paintings and Aaron Siskind Photographs, Holland-Goldosky Gallery, Chicago

1958   *Project I, Longview Foundation Purchases in Modern American Painting and Sculpture for the Union
Sanatorium Association of the International Ladies Garment Worker's Union,* Whitney Museum of
American Art, New York
Painting and Sculpture Acquisitions, Museum of Modern Art, New York

1957   *The 30s: Painting in New York,* Poindexter Gallery, New York
1957 Annual Exhibition: Sculpture, Paintings and Watercolor, Whitney Museum of American Art, New York
Group Show, March Gallery, New York
Museum Purchase Fund Collection, Syracuse Museum, Syracuse, New York (traveled)
U.S. Representation: Fourth International Art Exhibition, Metropolitan Art Gallery, Tokyo
Group Show, Tibor de Nagy Gallery, New York
Artists of the New York School: Second Generation Paintings by Twenty-Three Artists, Jewish Museum,
New York
Group Show, Tibor de Nagy Gallery, New York

1956   *Group Show,* Tanager Gallery, New York
Mid-Season Salon, Camino Gallery, New York
Fifth Annual Exhibition of Painting and Sculpture, The Stable Gallery, New York
Group Show, March Gallery, New York

1955   *Paintings, Sculpture,* Tanager Gallery, New York
Group Show, Poindexter Gallery, New York
The Stable Show, The Stable Gallery, New York

1954   *Third Annual Exhibition of Painting and Sculpture,* The Stable Gallery, New York

1953   *Group Show, Tanager Gallery,* New York
Second Annual Exhibition of Painting and Sculpture, The Stable Gallery, New York

1952   *Paintings–Sculpture,* Tanager Gallery, New York

1951   *9th Street Exhibition of Paintings and Sculpture,* 60 East 9th Street, New York

PUBLIC COLLECTIONS

Akron Art Museum, Ohio
Archer M. Huntington Art Gallery, University of Texas at Austin
The Art Museum, Princeton University, New Jersey
Australian National Gallery, Canberra
Birla Academy of Art and Culture, Calcutta, India
Carlson Gallery, University of Bridgeport College of Fine Arts, Connecticut
Cleveland Museum of Art, Ohio
College Union Collection, Wake Forest University, Winston-Salem, North Carolina
Fort Wayne Museum of Art, Indiana
Grey Art Gallery and Study Center, New York University, New York
Hampton University Museum, Virginia
Honolulu Academy of Arts, Hawaii
Hood Museum of Art, Dartmouth College, Hanover, New Hampshire
Jonson Gallery, University of New Mexico, Albuquerque
Madison Art Center, Wisconsin
Malmö Konsthall, Stockhom, Sweden
Metropolitan Museum of Art, New York
Milwaukee Art Museum, Wisconsin
Mint Museum of Art, Charlotte, NC
Modern Art Museum of Fort Worth, Texas
Museum of Modern Art, New York
National Gallery of Canada, Ottawa
National Gallery of Art, Washington, DC
National Museum of American Art, Smithsonian Institution, Washington, DC
Roswell Museum and Art Center, New Mexico
Santa Barbara Museum of Art, California
University of Nebraska; Lincoln/Sheldon Memorial Art Gallery and Sculpture Garden,
Lincoln, Nebraska
Solomon R. Guggenheim Museum, New York
University Art Museum and Pacific Film Archive, University of California, Berkeley
University of Iowa Museum of Art, Iowa City
Wexner Center for the Arts, Ohio State University, Columbus

Produced in an edition of 1,000 on the occasion of the exhibition

MILTON RESNICK

A Question of Seeing
Paintings 1959–1963

1 May through 7 June 2008

Designed by John Cheim

Essay © Nathan Kernan

Photography: *Burning Bush*, Digital Image © The Museum of Modern Art/Licensed by SCALA / Art Resource, NY; *Genie*, Geoffrey Clements; *East is the Place*, John Nienhuis; *Swan*, David Wharton; *Wedding*, Digital Image © The Metropolitan Museum of Art; all other works except *Mound*, Christopher Burke. Portraits of Milton Resnick: cover and spread following the essay: Resnick's Studio 811 Broadway c.1960 © Jesse Fernandez; frontispiece and spread in the biography: Resnick with *Swan*; spread before the essay, and second image in biography: Howard Wise Gallery opening 2/29/60 © Fred W. McDarrah; image before the biography: Milton Resnick and Pat Passlof at the Philip Gustion opening, Sydney Janis Gallery, 12/28/59 © Fred W. McDarrah.

Printed in the United States by GHP Media

ISBN 0-9797397-7-2

CHEIM & READ

547 West 25 Street New York